DUDLEY AND FRIENDS:

GRAND HARVEST BALL

Ellen Sherwood

Order this book online at www.trafford.com
or email orders@trafford.com

Most Trafford titles are also available at major online book retailers.

Printed in the United States of America.

ISBN: 978-1-4269-9353-4 (sc)
ISBN: 978-1-4269-9354-1 (e)

Trafford rev. 09/07/2011

www.trafford.com

North America & international
toll-free: 1 888 232 4444 (USA & Canada)
phone: 250 383 6864 ♦ fax: 812 355 4082

To: My Husband, Buck
My Son, David
My Daughter, Amy
My Grandchildren: Logan, Hunter,
Abigail, Allie, Malachi and Eli.
My Special Friend, Mary
My Sister, Edna
And my Mom, Lorene.

If I hadn't tried I wouldn't know the taste of success.

<u>Preface</u>

I started out with "Dudley and Friends" as my first book. I liked my characters so well that I wanted to continue writing about them. With help from friends and family this book came to be. I am continuing with the story.

Introduction

The humor continues. Dudley wants to liven things up a bit on the farm. With the help of Farmer Joe they have the Grandest Harvest Ball. Thus Dudley meets a special friend for life.

Dudley's Party For Old Timers

Dudley and Daisy lay sunning themselves beside the big lake. They had been married one year now and were very happy.

"Daisy, are you asleep?" Dudley asked.

"No Dudley, just resting my eyes," Daisy answered.

"We have got to have some excitement around here! Have you noticed that Simon Slick stays down at the barn sleeping all the time, and Farmer Joe hardly ever comes out of his house?" Dudley asked.

"Yes, Dudley. That is because they are getting older and they require more rest," Daisy said.

"Well, no matter how old I get, I am not going to lie around and be dull, dull all the time!" Dudley said.

"They can't help it, Dudley. Their bodies are wearing down and they need to rest more often or they wouldn't, uh, uh, uh." Daisy just didn't know how to say it.

"They wouldn't what, Daisy?" Dudley asked.

"They wouldn't be with us. They would have joined our parents by now," Daisy said.

"Are you sure, Daisy?" Dudley asked.

"I know for certain," Daisy answered.

Dudley lay there and thought for a moment then he said, "I am going for a walk, Daisy. I will be back soon."

Dudley got up and headed for the gate that took him from the big lake to the barn or to Farmer Joe's house. He looked back and saw Daisy going in for a swim. As much as he loved her, he couldn't imagine life without his other friends.

Dudley headed for Farmer Joe's house. When he reached the tree where Farmer Joe had married he and Daisy he saw Farmer Joe lying in a lawn chair under a tree in his yard. Dudley went to the fence and watched him for a moment, being careful not to wake him.

Dudley walked down the hill to the barn. He saw Simon Slick asleep on a soft pile of hay.

Dudley headed down the lane that took him to the back field. He met Delilah, the Dominecker hen. She was blind in one eye. She was hobbling along really slowly and mumbling something about being put in the pot. She didn't even notice Dudley. She just passed him by like he wasn't even there.

Dudley began to cry. " Is this what happens when we get old?" he asked. No wonder no one understands that this happens to older people and animals! How can they understand if someone doesn't tell them? They need me more than ever now!" Dudley said to himself.

Dudley walked all the way to the apple tree and turned around and saw the apple tree loaded with apples. It hit him that just like the apple tree put on new young sprouts and had plenty of apples it was up to the young to care for the older. If he and Simon Slick, and Daisy hadn't ate all the old apple sprouts, there wouldn't be any new ones. "Now Farmer Joe and Farmer Dan took good care of Simon Slick, Daisy, and myself. Farmer Joe even bought Daisy out of slavery for me. It doesn't matter what color or creed we all need someone to love us, and we all need to love someone, animals and humans. I know! I am going to have a party for my friends, and I am going to call it *The Party For Old Timers!*

Dudley headed up the lane. When he passed the barn Simon Slick was still sleeping. He went to Farmer Joe's house. Farmer Joe was still outside.

"Hello, Dudley," Farmer Joe said.

"Hello, Farmer Joe. How are you today?" Dudley asked.

"Well, I am fine. Thank you for asking," Farmer Joe replied.

"Farmer Joe, I want to have a party under the tree by the fence, Friday at four o'clock. It is a party for old timers. You invite your friends and Farmer Dan. I will bring Daisy and Simon Slick," Dudley announced.

"Ok, Dudley, we will meet under the big tree Friday at four o'clock. See you then!" Farmer Joe said.

Dudley told Simon Slick. He hadn't seen him this excited since they ate Farmer Joe's apples a year ago.

Daisy was excited! She asked Farmer Dan to bring shampoo and she and Dudley and Simon Slick had a bath in the big lake.

Dudley, Daisy, and Simon Slick got to the big tree. Farmer Joe had a tub filled with water sitting there. "What is that for?" Dudley asked.

"A game that we are going to play," Farmer Joe said.

A big, bright, red truck pulled up. Doctor Logan and Doctor Hunter got out.

"Let the party begin, Dudley!" Farmer Joe exclaimed.

Farmer Dan came walking up and joined them.

Dudley looked around. He didn't know where to start!

"Dudley, you begin," Farmer Joe said.

"Hello, everyone! I wanted to have this party today to discuss memories of where we have been and to create more memories because I want to make sure we have enough to last us a lifetime," Dudley said.

Everyone cheered! "Yea! Yea, Dudley!

Doctor Hunter clapped his hands and every person joined in.

"Back to Farmer Joe now," Dudley said.

"Farmer Joe had to clear his throat to speak. "I have organized some games for this party. We have *Horse Shoes, Apple Bobbing Contest, and The Watermelon Throwing Contest.* For refreshments we have: for Daisy, Dudley, and Simon Slick, corn pudding and apple cider, and for we gentlemen, tuna and ham sandwiches, chips and sodas. Ok! Let's party!" he said. "Who wants to throw a watermelon first?"

"I do!" Daisy yelled. She was embarrassed that no one else yelled.

Farmer Dan gave her a melon.

"Now, Daisy, you throw that melon as hard as you can from this line here. Whoever throws the melon the further is the winner," Farmer Dan said.

Daisy sucked in her breath and she drew back her head and swung as hard as she could! The melon sailed through the air and fell to the ground and popped into halves! Daisy stood looking stunned. "Can I eat that?" she asked.

"Of course you can, Daisy! We're having a party!" Farmer Joe said.

Daisy tested the melon. " This is as good as apples!" she said, and picked up half of the watermelon and moved away.

Farmer Dan marked where Daisy's melon had landed.

Simon Slick tried, but he came up shorter than Daisy.

Everyone took a turn. Dudley won the watermelon throwing contest.

"Ok, everyone, let's hear it for Dudley!" Farmer Joe said.

"Yea! Yea!" Simon Slick and Daisy yelled. All the people clapped and yelled, "Yea. Dudley!"

"Ok, Farmer Dan, help them play the apple bobbing contest," Farmer Joe said.

Farmer Dan poured apples into the tub as everyone watched.

"That looks like the apples I saw in the back field the other day," Dudley said.

" It is. I went and picked them early this morning," Farmer Dan said.

"Ok, listen up! In the apple bobbing contest you pick an apple up by the stem. Whoever gets the most apples wins. The men go first. It is better that way," Farmer Joe said.

Everyone laughed.

They all had taken a turn except Daisy and no one had gotten an apple yet.

"What do we do if Daisy doesn't get an apple, Farmer Joe?" Dudley asked.

"We have to change the water and wash the apples and try again," Farmer Joe said.

"I would rather call it a draw than have to do all that," Dudley said.

"Daisy looked at Dudley. "Do you think that because I am a girl that I can't do this?" she asked.

"No, Daisy, that's not what I mean at all! I am saying just in case you don't get an apple," Dudley said.

"Well, don't go planning my future for me, Dudley, until my past is finished! Ya hear?" Daisy said.

"Ok, Daisy," Dudley said.

"Boy!" Dudley thought, "for Daisy to be a white mule, she sure has a temper like a red-head! But that is why I love her. She is the prettiest white mule that I have ever seen."

Daisy had her head under the water. Doctor Logan and Doctor Hunter came over to observe. Daisy's head popped up and she was holding an apple between her teeth!

Farmer Joe cried, "Daisy's the winner of the apple bobbing contest!"

"I knew you could do it!" Dudley said.

Everyone cheered and clapped!

"Now you can eat the apples, but be careful and don't get sick!" Farmer Joe said.

"We will," Dudley, Daisy, and Simon Slick all said at the same time.

Everyone sat down to rest for a while.

"I would like to say something," Dudley announced. "Farmer Joe has always been good to us, so let's all share one of our favorite memories of him. Farmer Dan, you go first."

"I am glad to have this chance," Farmer Dan said, laughing.

"Uh oh!" Farmer Joe said. "I can tell that this is going to be a good one!"

"Well, Farmer Joe has always been good to us, but he hasn't always been good. Do you remember, Farmer Joe, when your two sisters came to visit and they made you so angry that you turned the outhouse over with them in it?" Farmer Dan asked.

"What is an outhouse?" Dudley asked.

"It is a building outside of a house called a bathroom. In your case, Dudley, it is where you go to relieve yourself," Farmer Joe answered. Farmer Joe began to laugh and everyone joined in.

"Well, why did you turn it over with them in it?" Dudley asked.

"They moved away to the city and they came back here trying to tell me how to run this farm. I figured that would send them packing back to their know it all friends," Farmer Joe said.

"Did they leave?" Daisy asked.

"In a hurry, after a good bath!" Farmer Joe said.

Everyone laughed for a few minutes and then became quiet.

"This reminds me of when my Mom and Dad were alive. Farmer Joe would joke with my Mom all the time. Farmer Joe, why was my Mom so special to you?" Dudley asked.

"Well, Dudley, she saved my life one time. I was cutting trees and one fell on me. Abigail got the tree off me and ran all the way back to the farm. She wouldn't stop pulling on Farmer Dan's shirt until he followed her back to me. She ran along the fence here by the house until Farmer Dan told her that I was going to be alright," Farmer Joe said.

"No wonder she was your favorite mule," Daisy said.

"No, She was my favorite Jenny," Farmer Joe said.

"Your what?" Dudley asked.

"Jenny," Farmer Joe said.

"My Mom was a white mule, like Daisy," Dudley said.

"No, your Mom was a Jenny and your Dad was a Jack-ass or you wouldn't be a mule," Farmer Joe said.

"Now you are telling me that I am a half breed, Farmer Joe?" Dudley asked.

"No, you are a mule. You only get a mule from a Jack- ass and a mare or a Jenny and a male horse. A Jenny is small and a Jack-ass is small. I picked your Dad special for your Mom," Farmer Joe said.

"Oh, well. It doesn't matter. I love them anyway. Isn't that what I am supposed to do, Daisy?" Dudley said.

"Yes, Dudley," Daisy said.

"Now let me tell you about Daisy. Her Dad was a mule and her Mom was a mule. Daisy is unique. She comes from a very rare breed, so Daisy is special. I have been watching her for a long time. The farmer that had her didn't know what he had when he sold her to Farmer Arlen and neither did Farmer Arlen. Daisy is a special breed and she is special to us," Farmer Joe said.

"She will always be special to me," Dudley said.

"Now, Simon Slick, your mom was a buggy horse mare, and your Dad was a Jack-ass. That is why you are bigger than Dudley and Daisy," Farmer Joe said.

"Gee, Farmer Joe, I didn't know that you knew my parents," Simon Slick said.

"Yes, you were born on my brother's farm. He sold you when you were first weaned to a man who didn't take care of his animals. One day that man put all of his animals up for sale. I found out that you were still there and I brought you here. Your parents had passed on by then. You are the prettiest black mule that I have ever laid eyes on," Farmer Joe replied.

"I am gonna cry if you keep this up, Farmer Joe," Simon Slick said.

"I was able to get your parents here on the farm but before I could get you, we lost them," Farmer Joe said.

Simon Slick looked at Farmer Joe for a long moment. "What happened to them?" he asked, but he didn't sound like himself.

"There was a barn in the back field at that time. One night some boys were hiding there from their parents and smoking cigarettes. They caught the barn on fire. Your parents were sleeping there. They died from smoke inhalation." Farmer Joe answered.

Simon Slick was crying. He couldn't speak. He cleared his throat. "Just give me a moment," he said.

"You're talking about my Aunt May May and Uncle Luke. I remember that," Dudley said.

"All of you have been in some bad situations. You are safe now, and free to roam my farm and do what you want, except eat my apples," Farmer Joe said.

"Don't worry! That potion we drank was enough to keep me away from that apple tree for the rest of my life!" Dudley said.

"What was that stuff that Doctor Hunter and Doctor Logan gave to us?" Simon Slick asked.

"That was linseed oil. I told Doctor Logan to see that you each got one quart. He said that would cure you, after some quality time in the bushes," Farmer Joe said.

"I am just glad that we got better. Why are you so good to us, Farmer Joe?" Daisy asked.

"Well, Daisy, when I was just a boy, my Dad would grow big fields of corn and make my brother and my sisters and myself work in it. We were made to hoe out weeds from right after daylight until right before sunset without food and water. We weren't allowed to stop for a break. If we complained, my Dad would take the bridle reins off the mule and beat us." Farmer Joe paused for a long moment.

Daisy, Dudley, and Simon Slick were all gasping for breath! They knew what bridle reins felt like!

"When I was ten years old, Farmer Malachi sent a card saying his family was coming for a visit. That's Farmer

Dan's Dad. When they arrived, my Dad tried to act nice, but he couldn't. He drank too much beer, so he became rude to Uncle Malachi. I saw that this was my chance to get out of this abuse. So, I told my cousin, Farmer Dan, that he was really mean to my brother, my sisters and myself. So Farmer Dan told Farmer Malachi that night. When he heard this, he had my Dad put in jail and took my Mom and all of us to safety. We went to live on Farmer Malachi's farm." Farmer Joe said.

There was a long pause. Everyone just sat there thinking about all they had heard.

"Tell us about Farmer Malachi." Dudley said.

"Well now, that Farmer Malachi had the best Harvest Ball anyone could throw."

"What is a Harvest Ball?" Daisy asked.

"Oh, when we gathered in all the food from the fields, Farmer Malachi would invite all his friends from Tennessee, where he was from, and Kentucky, where Doctor Logan's Dad lives, and Georgia, where Doctor Hunter's Dad lives, and Arkansas, which is where my brother lives. Everyone brought food and we danced and played games for three days. Everyone went home happy, healthy, and fed and everyone took sweet memories to carry with them through the cold winter," Farmer Joe said.

"Can we have a Harvest Ball, Farmer Joe?" Dudley asked.

"Well, yes, maybe. We will have to discuss it another time. My! My! Look at the time! It is getting late! Everyone needs to get home now," Farmer Joe said.

They all said good night and went home.

Dudley dreamed that night of having a beautiful Harvest Ball.

__Dudley Volunteers to Work__

Dudley woke up. The sun was shining brightly in his eyes.

"Boy was I tired, Daisy! Daisy?" Dudley said.

But Daisy wasn't there.

"Daisy!" Dudley said.

Dudley looked all around. He found her bathing in the big lake. He walked down to the edge of the lake where Daisy was.

"Good morning, Daisy," Dudley said.

"Good morning, Dudley! Come on in. It is going to be a beautiful day! Let's go for a swim!" Daisy said.

"Ok. Were you tired?" Dudley asked.

"Yes, but we had a wonderful time at the Old Timers Party, didn't we?" Daisy said.

"We sure did!" Dudley said.

"Are you coming into the lake, or not, Dudley? You look like you're in another world, the way you're standing there thinking so hard." Daisy said.

"Oh, no thanks, Daisy. I have to go talk to Farmer Joe. I'm sorry," Dudley said.

"Well, ok, Dudley. I will see you later," Daisy said.

Daisy swam out into the water.

Dudley headed for Farmer Joe's house. He forgot all about breakfast. What he had on his mind couldn't wait!

Farmer Dan met him coming up the hill. "Good morning, Dudley," Farmer Dan said.

"Good morning, Farmer Dan. Is Farmer Joe up yet?" Dudley asked.

"Yes. He is expecting you," Farmer Dan said.

Dudley looked at Farmer Dan but he didn't ask any questions. He knew that Farmer Joe had told farmer Dan what he planned to do.

Farmer Dan didn't say anything.

"Thanks, Farmer Dan," Dudley said.

Dudley went on to Farmer Joe's house. Farmer Joe was outside, waiting by the fence.

"Good morning, Dudley! How are you?" Farmer Joe asked.

"Fine, Farmer Joe," Dudley said.

There was an awkward pause.

Farmer Joe spoke. "Dudley, I have considered your request about the Harvest Ball. If I say yes, I will break my promise that I made to you and Simon Slick that you won't have to work anymore," he said.

"Not if I volunteer to work," Dudley said.

"Well, Simon Slick is up in his years and I understand about him. But what about Daisy?" Farmer Joe asked.

"She worked so hard as a slave. I can't do that to her. I have waited all my life for her. I love her more than anything. If I can do the crops myself, I am willing to work long, hard hours like I did at Farmer Frank's," Dudley said.

"Whoa! Whoa, Dudley! I will never work an animal as hard as he did! Not for any reason!" Farmer Joe said.

"Ok. I tried," Dudley said as he turned and started to walk away.

"Wait, Dudley. I didn't say no. Eight hours a day is all I think you should work," Farmer Joe said.

Dudley looked around at Farmer Joe and said, "Thank you, Farmer Joe. I knew you would find a way."

"Don't thank me. Thank Farmer Dan," Farmer Joe said.

"Farmer Dan? Why?" Dudley asked.

"He wanted to do this," Farmer Joe said.

"For me?" Dudley asked.

"No, not exactly. For Farmer Malachi, Farmer Dan's Dad. He wanted to do this for him, too. So do I. He raised me and he taught me everything I know about farming. I wouldn't have this farm if it wasn't for Farmer Malachi," Farmer Joe said.

"Wow, Farmer Joe! Where is Farmer Malachi?" Dudley asked.

"He lives here in Tennessee, Dudley," Farmer Joe said.

"Can he help us plan this Harvest Ball?" Dudley asked.

Farmer Joe looked heart broken and was quiet for so long that it scared Dudley.

Then he said, "No, Dudley. He is sick. He has to be cared for in a rest home. But he will come, to what I know is going to be the best Harvest Ball he has ever been to! Thanks to you, Dudley!"

"My pleasure! It is going to be the best Harvest Ball ever! I am going to work really hard, Farmer Joe!" Dudley said.

Farmer Joe was too emotional to talk so he nodded his head, yes.

"I forgot to eat breakfast. I am going to tell Simon Slick and Daisy!" Dudley said.

Dudley ran down the hill to the barn, expecting to find Simon Slick still sleeping. But to his surprise, Simon Slick was helping Farmer Dan move straw from in front of the machinery! Dudley was speechless!

"Dudley! Dudley! Did you hear the news? We are going to have a Harvest Ball! But first, there has to be a harvest," Simon Slick said.

"Yea! Isn't that great, Old Buddy? I am going to work this farm again and we will have a Harvest Ball!" Dudley said.

"Well, give me some credit here, too. I am going to work too," Simon Slick said.

"You can't do that! You're, you're tired all the time. You need your rest," Dudley said.

"One of my feet is not in the grave and the other one sliding on a skateboard yet! I am not too old. I slept because there was nothing to do on this cotton picking farm, Dudley," Simon Slick said.

"Dudley was shocked. He didn't know what to say. He looked over at Farmer Dan.

Farmer Dan motioned at him to just agree with Simon Slick.

"Ok, Old Buddy. Whatever you say," Dudley said.

Simon Slick was excited. He didn't even hear Dudley. He started singing, "I can get up every morning and go to work, when the work is done, I will dance the night away, until the wee hours of dawn. Simon Slick began to dance to the creek for a drink of water. Nothing could put a damper on his spirits today!

"Well, he sure is happy now," Dudley said.

"He sure is!" Farmer Dan said.

"How did it all happen this way?" Dudley asked.

"Well, Farmer Joe and I talked this over. We both knew that you and Simon Slick would volunteer to go to work. Who are you doing this for, Dudley?" Farmer Dan asked.

"For Farmer Joe, of course!" Dudley said.

"Well, Simon Slick said he is doing this for you," Farmer Dan stated. "Dudley, each and every one of us is doing this for ourselves and each other. You are bored to death and so is Simon Slick. Farmer Joe wants all of you to be happy and so do I. We knew what all of you would do as soon as you knew what a Harvest Ball was," Farmer Dan said.

"So when I asked if we could have a Harvest Ball, you knew that we would have to go to work?" Dudley asked.

"Exactly," Farmer Dan said.

"Well, I am glad! It will be the best Harvest Ball ever! You just wait and see!" Dudley said.

"My Father, Farmer Malachi, will love this, in his old age," Farmer Dan said.

"How old is Farmer Malachi?" Dudley asked.

"One hundred and one years old, this fall. Isn't that something?" Farmer Dan asked.

"That's something, alright! I am still young and so is Simon Slick. We have work to do, now. When do we start?" Dudley asked.

"We will get the machinery ready today and start tomorrow," Farmer Dan said.

Dudley and Simon Slick worked hard to get ready for the next day.

Meanwhile, Farmer Joe took a trip down the road from the farm to see an old friend of his, Mary Brown.

When Mary answered the door she was surprised to see Farmer Joe.

"Hello, Mary. How have you been?" Farmer Joe asked.

"Fine. Come in and have a seat and tell me what is on your mind!" Mary said.

Mary had been Farmer Malachi's cook and housekeeper and everyone loved her like she was part of the family.

"Well, Mary, I need you," Farmer Joe said.

"Me! Now what do you need me for?" Mary asked.

Farmer Joe told her what was going on. "It will be just like old times when you and I danced until midnight, before Farmer Malachi got sick." Farmer Joe added.

"Well, that was a long time ago. But it tugs at these old heart strings of mine to do this again and see everyone again," Mary said.

"It will be an experience that we will never forget. When can you start?" Farmer Joe asked.

"Tomorrow afternoon. I can stay at your place and come home for the weekends," Mary said.

"Ok. I will be here tomorrow evening," Farmer Joe said.

"See you then," Mary said.

It was going to be like home, having Mary around. She had worked for Farmer Malachi since she was young. She was a wonderful cook and housekeeper.

When Farmer Joe turned up the drive to his house, he saw all the machinery lined up in a row down by the barn. Farmer Dan, Daisy, Dudley and Simon Slick sat in the end of the barn, taking a break.

"Boy, they have been busy!" Farmer Joe said.

Daisy saw Farmer Joe get out of his truck.

"Dudley, I am going up the hill and tell Farmer Joe that I am going to work tomorrow," Daisy said.

"Ok, Daisy," Dudley said.

Daisy walked up the hill.

Farmer Joe was leaning against the fence looking over the farm.

"Hey, Farmer Joe. How are you?" Daisy asked.

"Fine, thank you, Daisy," Farmer Joe said.

"It sure is a nice spring day," Daisy said.

"Yes, it is nice for working the farm," Farmer Joe said.

"Yeah. I want to work, too," Daisy said.

"Hmm," Farmer Joe said.

"I could relieve Dudley or Simon Slick once in a while," Daisy pleaded.

"What about Dudley? He would be worried about you?" Farmer Joe asked.

"Oh, that," Daisy said. She paused for a moment. "I told Dudley that I needed to feel needed and if I had to sit and do nothing would be just as bad as being a slave. But this way I won't be worked to death either."

"Well, if it is ok with Dudley that you work, it is ok with me, too," Farmer Joe said.

"Good. We start tomorrow," Daisy said.

"You mean you're ready tomorrow? Looks like Dudley and Simon Slick have put in a pretty good day," Farmer Joe said.

They both looked toward the barn a moment.

"Thank you, Farmer Joe. I'd better go back. They might need me," Daisy said.

"Oh, Daisy, keep it safe now, you hear?" Farmer Joe said.

"Ok, Farmer Joe," Daisy said.

Daisy ran down the hill to the barn.

"Ok, we meet here tomorrow," Farmer Dan said just as Daisy reached them.

Farmer Dan went toward Farmer Joe's house.

Dudley, Daisy, and Simon Slick went toward the big lake.

"What did Farmer Joe say, Daisy?" Dudley asked.

"He said that if it is ok with you for me to work, that it is ok with him. Oh, and keep it safe," Daisy said.

"Fine," Dudley said.

"This is going to be fun!" Simon Slick said.

Simon Slick pushed Dudley into the big lake and went in after him.

"Old Buddy, you have had it now," Dudley said and pushed him back.

"The two of you, listen to me! Be careful and don't get hurt or you can't work tomorrow!" Daisy said.

"Listen to her! Nag! Nag! Nag! Shall we?" Simon Slick said.

They were talking very low so Daisy couldn't hear them.

"We shall," Dudley said.

They both began walking very slowly out of the water.

"It is about time you listened to me," Daisy said. They had reached her by this time.

"Are you going for a swim, Daisy?" Dudley asked.

"After awhile," Daisy said.

Simon Slick was bursting.

"Daisy, you and I have been friends since you came here, right?" Simon Slick said.

"Why, yes, we have," Daisy said.

"Enough for me to give you a simple, well, a simple…" Simon Slick said. He puckered up his lips and closed his eyes.

Daisy did the same thing.

"Bath time!" Simon Slick said. He and Dudley pushed her into the big lake!

"Now look what the two of you have done! You got me all wet!" Daisy said.

"That's what we meant to do," Dudley said.

Dudley and Simon Slick went back into the water, laughing.

Daisy began to laugh too.

"This feels good," Daisy said.

"Which one? The water or the laughing?" Dudley asked.

"Both," Daisy answered.

"Yeah. It's been a long time since we laughed like this!" Simon Slick said.

"This is good for us," Daisy said.

"Dudley, you have given me something to live for, and a life to look forward to, by suggesting to Farmer Joe that we have a Harvest Ball. This is your best idea yet!" Simon Slick said.

"Yes, it is! You won't hate me when you're out there sweating in the hot sun, will you?' Daisy asked.

"No, it will be good for us," Dudley said.

"Yes, and it gives us something to look forward to," Simon Slick said.

"I am going to remind you of what you said if either of you ever get angry with me," Dudley said.

"Ok, Dudley," Simon Slick said.

They played around in the water for a little while.

"I am getting out," Daisy said.

"Why, Daisy? You have not been in here long," Dudley said.

"I am just very tired," Daisy said.

"You're tired from watching us work? Well you won't last a day," Simon Slick said.

Dudley and Simon Slick laughed as Daisy walked onto the bank.

"She will be alright," Dudley said.

"We all will once we get back in shape," Simon Slick said.

"Well, I guess we had better get out of here. It will be dark soon and we all need a good night's sleep," Dudley said.

" I had better go eat and take my place down by the barn," Simon Slick said.

"Simon Slick, your place is here, with me and Daisy," Dudley said.

"Well, I thought you wanted privacy," Simon Slick said.

"Simon Slick, if we want privacy we will tell you. Better yet, we can go down by the barn if we want privacy," Dudley said.

They both laughed and walked out of the big lake together. They all went to the barn to eat.

Up on the hill, Farmer Joe was sitting down to eat supper. Farmer Dan was joining him.

"You went to see Mary Brown today, didn't you?" Farmer Dan asked.

"And what is wrong with that?" Farmer Joe asked.

Farmer Joe had a big smile on his face.

"Well, now let me see? Now, Joe, you know you can't keep a secret from me. I know that you're sweet on her," Farmer Dan said.

"Well, you'd better be quiet about it, because she is coming here to stay except weekends until after the Harvest Ball," Farmer Joe said.

"That means that there is going to be some good food around here," Farmer Dan said.

"Now you had better mind your manners, Farmer Dan," Farmer Joe said.

"You will have her cooking, canning, and preserving for you. Oh, and cleaning. Watch out. When she finds out how dirty you can get, she will run all the way home." Farmer Dan said.

Everyone knows that she is the best cook in Tennessee, Kentucky, and Georgia all put together. She will take care of the food from the harvest just fine," Farmer Joe said.

"You got me there. She is a really good cook, one of the best. And she is good to everyone. Yes, Mary Brown sure has a good heart," Farmer Dan said.

"There has never been an old, tired, hungry soul in better hands than Mary's. She is as good as gold," Farmer Joe said.

Farmer Dan did the dishes and told Farmer Joe good night and went home.

After Farmer Dan left, Farmer Joe went to the sliding glass door and looked out across the farm. He remembered what it had looked like with all the fields planted. He thought about how nice it would be to have Mary around again and the changes she would make once she got a hold of this old place. He knew that it would come alive again. He thought about Daisy, Dudley, and Simon Slick. They had given him a reason to go on. He spoke toward the big lake where Dudley lay sleeping and said, "Thank you, Dudley."

Dudley dreamed that he was looking at the farm. Everything was planted. He turned to look toward Farmer Joe's house. He saw Farmer Joe standing on the porch with a woman. They were waving and he heard Farmer Joe say," Thank you, Dudley."

"Thank you, Farmer Joe," Dudley said.

Dudley's Planting of The Seeds

Daylight was peeking through the clouds. Dudley opened his eyes. He remembered that this was the big day!

"Wake up! Wake up! Wake up, everybody! It's time to get up and get ready for work!" Dudley said.

Dudley stood up. Daisy stretched.

"Today we get to plow and plant the seeds for the grandest harvest of all!" Daisy said.

Simon Slick groaned and stood up. "I am ready," he said, and started to walk to the barn. But he was limping.

"What's wrong with your leg, Simon Slick?" Dudley asked.

"I don't know. Sometimes I am sore. But it goes away after I walk a little," Simon Slick said.

"You can't work like that!" Daisy said.

"No, you need to see a doctor," Dudley said.

"Ok, Dudley. I am sorry. I hurt pretty badly today," Simon Slick said.

"Don't apologize. It's not your fault. I am going to get Farmer Dan," Dudley said.

Dudley headed for the barn to get Farmer Dan. He found him putting food out for them to eat.

"Farmer Dan, something is wrong with Simon Slick's leg. He needs a doctor," Dudley said.

"I will tell Farmer Joe to call the doctor. You and Daisy go ahead and eat. I will take some food to Simon Slick," Farmer Dan said.

Farmer Dan went to Farmer Joe's house and Dudley went back to the big lake where Simon Slick and Daisy were.

"Farmer Dan is gone to tell Farmer Joe to call the doctor, Simon Slick," Dudley said.

"Good. Maybe I can work after all," Simon Slick said.

"Now don't you go worrying about that, Old Buddy. Daisy and I have that covered. You just get better," Dudley said.

"Ok, Dudley. I will try not to worry," Simon Slick said.

"Good. Daisy and I have to go eat but Farmer Dan is going to bring you something to eat," Dudley said.

"Ok, Dudley. Thank you," Simon Slick said.

Dudley and Daisy headed for the barn. They met Farmer Dan bringing food to Simon Slick.

"Doctor Wiley is right down the road. He is coming to take a look at Simon Slick's leg," Farmer Dan said.

Dudley and Daisy ate and went to see which machinery Farmer Dan wanted to hook them to.

"Are you ready?" Farmer Dan asked.

"Yes!" Dudley answered.

"Yes!" Daisy answered.

"Ok, let's do this!" Farmer Dan said.

He paused a moment and Dudley saw a tear in his eye.

"Just back right up here, Dudley," Farmer Dan said.

Dudley backed up and Farmer Dan put a bridle on him. Then Farmer Dan hooked two things that looked like leather straps to the sides of the bridle. These two things are called bridle reins. The reins pulled on an object in Dudley's mouth called a bit.

"I don't like these things in my mouth," Dudley said.

"I don't either," Daisy said.

Farmer Dan put a harness on Dudley and securely buckled it under his belly. It looked like an oversized belt.

"Now we are going to be on our way soon," Dudley said.

Farmer Dan finished hooking Dudley to the plow. He did the same with Daisy.

"We are ready to go now," Farmer Dan said.

"Farmer Dan, when we get to the field, I want to do a groundbreaking ceremony," Dudley said.

"Gitty up!" Farmer Dan said.

Dudley and Daisy began to pull the plow. They headed for the field.

"It sure is a nice day for plowing," Daisy said.

"It sure is," Dudley said.

Farmer Joe had gotten up before dawn and drove by Mary Brown's house. He saw a light on and thought something might be wrong so he stopped to check on her.

"Oh, I am just fine. I couldn't sleep for thinking about all of the upcoming events that are going to be taking place on your farm," Mary told him.

"And that is why I am out driving around before dawn," Farmer Joe said.

"Well, I have a wonderful idea," Mary said.

"And what is that?" Farmer Joe asked.

"Since I am packed and ready to go, why don't we load up my things and go to your place and I will cook up some breakfast for you," Mary said.

So, there on the hill stood Farmer Joe with Mary at his side watching as Dudley and Daisy pulled the turning plow into the field and stopped.

"Ok, Dudley, go ahead," Farmer Dan said.

Everyone paused for a moment.

"God, we thank you for giving us the chance to prepare the soil and plant the seeds, and may we reap a bountiful harvest. Bless Farmer Malachi, and Farmer Joe, and Farmer Dan, and all of us that are here today," Dudley prayed. Dudley paused.

"Go, Farmer Dan," Dudley said.

Daisy and Dudley pulled the plow and it buried into the soil.

Farmer Joe choked back the tears and Mary patted him on the back.

Farmer Dan just let his tears flow freely down his face as he walked along behind the plow.

And Simon Slick, who had been given a shot and had horse liniment rubbed on his leg was standing behind a bush added, "Bless my buddy, Dudley, who thinks of everyone else but himself, Amen."

"It feels so good to see this old farm up and running! I just wish that I was out there working, too," Farmer Joe said.

"You will be. You will be!" Mary said. But her mind had wandered back to a time when the love of her life had slipped away in a single second. She had vowed to herself that if given that chance again, he wouldn't slip away again.

Dudley and Daisy worked hard plowing the field. Daisy taught Dudley a song she knew when she was very young. "Around the field we will go, and plow another furrow, plant a seed and pull some weeds, and watch our garden grow!" Daisy sang.

"Where did you learn that?" Dudley asked.

"My Mom," Daisy said.

"You never talk much about your parents," Dudley said.

"My Mom stayed on the farm with me until I was a year old. She was sold. My Dad was already gone when I was born," Daisy said.

"Boy, you were so young!" Dudley said.

"The song is all I have left of my Mom. She sang it to me in the field when she was working, to pass the time. She told me so," Daisy said.

"Well, we will just have to do what Farmer Joe said. Create enough memories to last a lifetime," Dudley said.

"Yeah. I wonder how Simon Slick is," Daisy said.

"I think he is feeling better. I saw him over by the gate in the bushes a while ago," Dudley said.

"He knows that he is not supposed to be up on his leg, but he had to come and see us working," Daisy said.

"Whoa!" Farmer Dan said.

Dudley and Daisy stopped.

"Ok. We will come back in an hour and we are ready to plant the seeds in this field," Farmer Dan said.

"Alright. Let's go tell Simon Slick, Daisy," Dudley said.

Dudley and Daisy hurried to the big lake.

"How are you, Old Buddy?" Dudley asked.

"I am a lot better. I think that I am well enough to work this afternoon," Simon Slick said.

"Oh no you don't!" Daisy said so firmly that even Dudley looked at her.

"You need to rest. You can start tomorrow," Dudley said.

Daisy was not happy that Simon Slick's leg was hurt, but she secretly wished that he would take just one more day and let her work beside Dudley. Daisy had felt like a million dollars out there in that field with Dudley.

The time passed swiftly and it was time to go back to work.

Dudley was beside himself with excitement.

"Farmer Dan, can I drop the first seed?" Dudley asked.

"Considering that I only need one of you at a time to pull the corn planter, you can go first, Dudley," Farmer Dan said.

"No, I want to put one corn seed in the soil first," Dudley said.

"Ok, Dudley. We can do that," Farmer Dan said.

Farmer Dan put a seed in Dudley's mouth and instructed him where to drop it.

Dudley dropped the seed in the row and cheers went up all around him!

Farmer Joe and Mary cheered at the house!

Delilah cheered at the barn!

Daisy and Dudley cheered with Farmer Dan!

Dudley and Daisy took turns pulling the corn planter that evening. They finished the field of corn.

"We will go to the back field and start back there tomorrow," Farmer Dan said.

"See you bright and early tomorrow, Farmer Dan," Dudley said.

"Bye, Farmer Dan," Daisy said.

Dudley and Daisy hurried to the barn to eat and went to check on Simon Slick.

Farmer Dan went up the hill to Farmer Joe's house. When he walked into the house he smelled an aroma that brought back a lot of memories.

"Let me guess! Pot roast, green beans, mashed potatoes smothered in your famous gravy, and hot apple pie with a little nutmeg and ice cream for dessert. Oh, and Mary's number one rolls," Farmer Dan said to Mary.

"Well, you either have a good nose or a great memory," Mary said.

"I would say a little of both. After all, it is Farmer Joe's and my favorite meal," Farmer Dan said.

"Go wash up and we will eat," Mary said.

"I will right away," Farmer Dan said.

As Farmer Dan went through the den, he saw Farmer Joe sitting on the porch.

"Farmer Joe, do you know what Mary has made for supper?" Farmer Dan asked.

"I sure do. I peeled the potatoes and the apples for her," Farmer Joe said.

"You have not peeled potatoes or apples in a long time! Are you still sweet on Mary Brown after all these years?" Farmer Dan asked.

"Well a man can help a woman can't he? Mind your own business now, Farmer Dan!" Farmer Joe said.

"Ok! Ok! Don't get upset! I was just asking," Farmer Dan said.

"Go on and wash up for supper now. I will meet you at the table," Farmer Joe said.

When Farmer Dan disappeared into the hall, Farmer Joe shook his head and let out a sigh. "Boy, Farmer Dan doesn't miss a thing, does he?" Farmer Joe said to himself.

"What doesn't Farmer Dan miss?" Mary asked.

Farmer Joe turned around and she was standing in the doorway.

"Oh, Mary, I didn't know you were there. I was just talking to myself," Farmer Joe answered.

"Well you'd better watch what you say to Self. Someone might be listening," Mary said.

They both laughed.

Farmer Joe stood and walked over to the door. "Let's go test that fine meal that you have prepared for us," he said.

Farmer Joe put his arm around Mary and they walked to the dining room together. Farmer Joe adjusted Mary's chair for her and helped her sit down. He turned to take his seat when Farmer Dan came in, smiling.

Dudley, Daisy and Simon Slick lay on the grass by the big lake watching the sun go down.

"When did the doctor say you could go back to work, Simon Slick," Dudley asked.

"Tomorrow, and boy am I glad, too," Simon Slick said.

"Well, Daisy, it looks like you will get the day off," Dudley said.

"I will find something to do," Daisy said.

Dudley heard a noise. Ber-shew, Ber-shew. He looked around to find Simon Slick asleep and snoring.

"We are the ones who worked so hard, and look who's sleeping," Dudley said.

"Wake him up and tell him that he is snoring too loud. Tell him to stay awake until we go to sleep, because he is keeping us awake," Daisy said.

"Why, Daisy, I wouldn't have thought about you being so funny," Dudley said.

About that time, Simon Slick snored loudly. Dudley and Daisy both looked at on another, then at Simon Slick for a moment.

"Good idea," Dudley said.

Dudley leaned over to Simon Slick's ear and cleared his throat. Simon Slick grunted.

"Simon Slick. Oh, Simon Slick," Dudley said.

Simon Slick raised his head. "Wh, wh,What, t, time to get up? I am going," he said.

"You're snoring very loudly. Daisy and I can't sleep. Will you just stay awake long enough for us to get to sleep, then go to sleep? That won't bother us," Dudley said.

"Ok. Ok," Simon Slick said.

Daisy and Dudley both lay down their heads and they were out like a light being turned off.

Simon Slick listened for their breathing to change so he would know when they were asleep.

Dudley started dreaming of running through a field. Daisy was chasing him. She caught him and Dudley laughed at her. Dudley did not know that he had laughed out loud in his sleep.

Simon Slick heard Dudley laugh out. "Why, you! I will get the two of you for this, I promise," Simon Slick said.

Simon Slick went to sleep. The next morning he woke up early and walked down to the barn.

Farmer Dan was feeding the animals. He put oats out in buckets, one each for Simon Slick, Dudley, and Daisy. Simon Slick ate his food and watched Farmer Dan finish with his chores.

"I am going to eat breakfast. Tell the others that we will start when I get back," Farmer Dan said.

Farmer Dan went to Farmer Joe's house and Simon Slick went back to the big lake.

Simon Slick heard a truck and looked up at Farmer Joe's house. A big truck was backing to the gate in the driveway.

Dudley and Daisy came walking up to Simon Slick.

"What is going on?" Dudley asked Simon Slick.

About that time, a cow jumped out of the truck and ran down the hill.

"Well that is what is going on. A cow has come to live with us," Simon Slick said.

"She is coming over here," Daisy said.

She came to a stop about three feet from Dudley. She announced, "My name is Beth. Who are you?"

"My name is Dudley. This is my friend, Simon Slick. And this is my wife, Daisy," Dudley said.

"You have got to be kidding! Two mules got married? I have heard some strange things in my lifetime. This has to top them all!" Beth said.

"What's wrong with that?" Dudley asked.

"You will know when another pretty mule comes your way and you can't get rid of the wifey," Beth said.

"He is not like that," Daisy said.

"We will see," Beth said.

"No, he is not like that!" Simon Slick said.

"And I thought you were the smart one, Simon Slick," Beth said. "Well, let me check this place out, since I am going to live here.

Beth went on down to the big lake.

Dudley, Daisy, and Simon Slick went to the barn to get ready to start their day.

"What am I going to do? I don't want to spend the day with Beth. She sounds mean!" Daisy said.

"You will be alright. She is just a cow," Dudley said.

Farmer Dan arrived and was ready to go to work.

"Don't worry about Beth. She will be alright, once she calms down," Farmer Dan said.

"Why is she so upset?" Dudley asked.

"She was taking care of some baby calves on the farm that she came from. They had to be separated. She cried and said that they were taking her babies away," Farmer Dan said.

"Oh, how sad! The poor thing!" Daisy said.

"I understand now," Dudley said.

"Me, too," Daisy and Simon Slick both said at the same time.

Dudley and Simon Slick worked hard that day. Daisy brought them drinking water in a bucket. Mary gave Daisy a thermos bottle to take to Farmer Dan. Farmer Dan enjoyed the good, cold water and told Daisy that she deserved a medal for that.

Beth lay down by the barn all day.

When they finished that day, Farmer Dan made an announcement. "Tomorrow all the seeds will be planted!" Farmer Dan said.

"We will soon have all the seeds planted, and we can watch our harvest grow!" Dudley said.

"Yea! Yea!" they all cried.

When they turned around to go to the barn, Beth was standing behind them. "I'm glad somebody is happy," she said and walked away.

"Beth! Beth!" Daisy said. But Beth didn't stop or look back.

"It is alright, Daisy. There is probably nothing you can do anyway," Dudley said.

They all went to eat and went to bed early.

Dudley and Simon Slick worked hard and Daisy carried water faithfully.

Beth stayed down by the barn, only talking when she had to.

Soon all the seeds were planted and it was time to rest until the harvest time!

Dudley's Grand Harvest

Farmer Joe had told them that it was time to cut the hay and put it in the barn.

"How do we cut the hay and put it in the barn, Simon Slick?" Dudley asked.

"Well, I have never worked in hay but I have watched," Simon Slick said.

"You have?" Dudley asked.

"First we will pull a mowing machine over the field and cut all the hay down. Then, the hay has to dry for a few days. Farmer Dan will hook us to a hay rake and we will rake the hay up in rows," Simon Slick explained to Dudley.

"You boys ready?" Farmer Dan yelled.

"We're coming!" Dudley said.

Farmer Dan hooked them to the mowing machine and they mowed all the hay, only stopping when Daisy brought them cold water.

"That's not too bad," Dudley said.

"Not yet," Simon Slick said.

"I am tired. I believe I will sleep good tonight," Dudley said.

That night they were all lying beside the big lake and Dudley asked something that they all had been thinking. "Why did Farmer Joe buy Beth and bring her here away from her babies?" he asked.

"I don't know. I have never known Farmer Joe to do such a thing," Simon Slick said.

They heard a strange noise down by the barn.

"Listen!" Daisy said.

"It sounds like Beth is dying!" Dudley said.

Dudley sprang to his feet and headed toward the barn.

"Oh no! Oh no! Farmer Joe has caused her to grieve herself to death!" Dudley said.

When he got there, Beth was stretched out on her side making a terrible noise. Dudley looked down into her face.

"Beth, don't give up and die! We will help you," Dudley said.

"I'm not dying, I just need a doctor," Beth said.

"Ok," Dudley said.

Dudley turned and ran for Farmer Joe's house as fast as he could go. He passed Daisy and Simon Slick and jumped the fence at Farmer Joe's house. He ran up and kicked the door. Dudley meant for someone to hear him quickly!

Farmer Joe came rushing to the door and turned on the porch light. He saw Dudley and opened the door.

"What is going on, Dudley?" Farmer Joe asked.

"Beth needs a doctor!" Dudley said.

"Ok. I will call Doctor Logan," Farmer Joe said.

Farmer Joe disappeared into his house for a few minutes. "Doctor Logan is on his way," Farmer Joe said when he returned.

Dudley just stood there looking at Farmer Joe.

"What is it , Dudley? What is wrong?" Farmer Joe asked.

"Farmer Joe, why did you buy Beth and take her away from all her babies?" Dudley asked.

"Her babies were already sold when I bought her. I bought her so that she could keep the one she is going to have tonight." Farmer Joe said.

Dudley was speechless! He stood there with his mouth hanging open and just stared at Farmer Joe.

"Of course you did! I should have known! You've always been good to animals," Dudley said.

Dudley was so ashamed. He hung his head.

"I am sorry, Farmer Joe," Dudley said.

They stood there in silence for a moment.

"I'd better get back and tell Beth," Dudley said.

Dudley started toward the fence and Farmer Joe spoke, "Dudley, I should have told you, and there wouldn't be this big misunderstanding. I am not upset with you for what you were thinking. Thank you, Dudley," Farmer Joe said.

Dudley looked at Farmer Joe for a long moment. "Thank you, Farmer Joe. I should be thanking you!" Dudley said.

Dudley turned and ran and jumped the fence. He felt like a million bucks! He might as well have been a million bucks as far as Farmer Joe was concerned!

Dudley ran down the hill and around the barn to Beth.

"Ok! Ok! Everyone give Beth some room to breathe. Doctor Logan is on the way! Beth is going to be a Mamma tonight!" Dudley said.

"I am?" Beth asked. That explains this terrible pain in my belly!" Beth said and laughed.

Daisy saw Doctor Logan's truck lights at the top of the hill. "Here is Doctor Logan," Daisy said.

Simon Slick stood away from the others. He whispered, "Oh, the miracle of birth!" He was crying. He knew that this was just what Beth needed. He knew what Farmer Joe had done. "What a wonderful man!" Simon Slick said.

Doctor Logan appeared beside Beth. "How are you?" he asked her.

"Fine," Beth said.

"Well, if that's the way it is, you don't need me. I can go home and get a good night's sleep," Doctor Logan said.

"No, no! I just meant that I was fine considering I am about to give birth," Beth said.

"That's what I thought," Doctor Logan said.

"Alright everyone! Let's give Beth some privacy," Dudley said.

Everyone followed Dudley and Daisy to the big lake.

"Gee, I wanted to watch," Simon Slick said and laughed at Dudley.

"Shame on you, Simon Slick!" Daisy said.

"Might as well laugh as to cry," Simon Slick said.

They remained quiet for a while.

"I don't hear anything, anymore. Do you think that everything is alright?" Dudley asked.

"I was thinking the same thing," Daisy said.

They all started for the barn. They heard Doctor Logan say, "Ok, everyone. Beth is a Mom!"

They ran the rest of the way and all came to a stop at Beth's feet.

"Wow! Look at this, Beth! You really are a Mom, aren't you?!" Dudley said.

"I sure am a proud one, too!" Beth said.

Beth didn't just have one calf that night. She had two, a set of twins as white as snow. She named one Cotton and the other one Little Joe, after the farmer who gave her everything she could wish for. She would see her babies grow up here and have families of their own.

They all slept peacefully that night.

Dudley talked about Cotton and Little Joe until he fell asleep.

Dudley, Daisy and Simon Slick saw a different Beth. She turned out to be kind and lovable after all.

The excitement was awesome the next morning.

Farmer Joe and Mary came down to the barn to tell Beth how beautiful her babies were.

Mary told everyone to come to the big tree that evening for a celebration.

All the animals lined up under the big tree that evening.

Farmer Joe came out of the house carrying a big bowl of corn on the cob. Mary was right behind him with a big bowl.

"What is that?" Daisy asked.

"Potato salad," Mary said.

"It looks good," Dudley said.

Farmer Dan came out carrying a large plate with a bowl in the middle.

"I know what those things are. They are carrots," Dudley said.

"How do you know?" Daisy asked.

"Farmer Joe gave them to my Mom to give to me when I was little," Dudley said.

"This is lettuce, cucumber, radish, tomato, and green onion," Farmer Dan said.

"And that bowl in the middle is Mary's famous farm dip," Farmer Joe said.

Everyone gathered around the table and Farmer Joe said the blessing and thanked God for Beth's new babies and asked God to always protect them. Everyone began to eat and Farmer Joe and Mary excused themselves.

"Where did they go? Don't they want to eat with us?" Dudley asked.

"Yes, they are going to eat with us. They have gone to get something," Farmer Dan said.

They all got busy complimenting the food and didn't hear Farmer Joe and Mary until they were almost to the table.

"Wow!" Daisy said. "What a big uh, uh…"

"Apple cobbler," Mary said.

"I know that I am going to eat some of that!" Dudley said.

"This is for dessert," Farmer Joe said.

"What does that mean?" Beth asked.

"When we finish all the food that is good for us, then we can have some that is not as good for us," Dudley said.

"Some desserts are good for you. In this case you have to be careful and not eat too much sugar," Mary said.

"Oh? A little boy gave me a lump of sugar one time," Daisy said.

"Is everyone ready for dessert, now?" Farmer Dan said.

"Yes!" they all said at the same time.

They all began to eat the apple cobbler.

"Yum, good!" Dudley said.

"Oh my!" Simon Slick said.

"This is the best food that I have ever tasted!" Daisy said.

"I will never forget this! No one has ever b-b-been th-this n-nice to m-m-me." Beth said. She was crying tears of joy. She truly had found a home!

"Beth, this is your home and we are glad to have you and your babies here. Enjoy your life to the fullest," Farmer Joe said.

"Those two babies of yours are the prettiest calves that I have ever seen," Mary said.

"Thank you, Mary," Beth said.

"Ok everybody! Better eat up! Dudley and Simon Slick have to work in the hay tomorrow," Farmer Joe said.

They all finished eating and did what they could to clean up. They all went to prepare for bed.

"Simon Slick, will you tell me how we will do the hay tomorrow?" Dudley asked.

Dudley, Daisy and Simon Slick all got a drink of water and lay down in their favorite spots.

"What do you want to know?" Simon Slick asked.

"What do we do next?" Dudley asked.

"First we will rake the hay up in rows. Then Farmer Dan will hook us to a wagon. You will be on one side of the row of hay and I will be on the other side. The wagon will have a hay loader hooked behind it. Two people have to be on the wagon, Farmer Dan and Farmer Joe's friend, Paul, from the farm down the road. There are leather straps called guide lines that will hook to each side of our bridles and run back to Paul. He will lead us where we need to go," Simon Slick said.

"I know about those lines and how they will hurt if you get a whipping with them! We learned that at Farmer Frank's," Dudley said.

"We sure did!" Simon Slick said.

"Sometimes Paul will help Farmer Dan pack the hay on the wagon. When the wagon is full he will unhook the loader and we will go put the hay in the barn," Simon Slick said.

There was a long pause.

"Simon Slick, how do two people work on a wagon with pitch forks and not knock each other off?" Dudley asked.

Simon Slick laughed. "Farmer Dan will get on the back of the wagon and Paul will get on the front. We will be going slowly. Believe me, Dudley, we won't be running any races with all that weight behind us," Simon Slick said.

"Boy! This sure sounds hard!" Dudley said.

"We'd better get some sleep. We have to get up early," Simon Slick said.

"Good night, Daisy, Simon Slick," Dudley said.

"Good night," Daisy and Simon Slick said at the same time.

The next morning they got up bright and early. There was no dew on the grass so they started working very early.

When they hauled the first load of hay to the barn Daisy came carrying a cold bucket of water.

Farmer Dan unhooked Simon Slick and Dudley from the wagon. "We will take a break here. I will yell for you in a little while," he said.

Dudley and his friends went and ate. They all lay down by the big lake to rest.

"Do you want me to work this afternoon and let you rest, Dudley?" Daisy asked.

"No, Daisy. That wagon is hard to pull, especially when it is loaded down with hay," Dudley said.

Dudley paused. "Poor Daisy. She would do anything to help me," he thought.

"Simon Slick and I will get the hay, Daisy," Dudley said.

"Yeah, Daisy, it is hard work," Simon Slick said.

"Well, I can work hard," Daisy said.

"Now, Daisy, thank you. But I don't want you to have to work like this. You just bring us water and we will do alright," Dudley said.

"Well, ok, if you're sure," Daisy said.

They rested a while and took a swim in the big lake to cool off.

They heard Farmer Dan call, "Dudley and Simon Slick, time to go back to work."

Dudley and Simon Slick went to the barn.

"Do you boys see that fork there?" Farmer Dan asked.

Dudley looked up in the barn loft at a hay fork.

"Yes, Farmer Dan," Simon Slick said.

"What about you, Dudley?" Farmer Dan asked.

"Yes, but that's not a fork. I saw Farmer Joe eating on his porch one day and his fork didn't look like that," Dudley said.

Farmer Dan laughed. "Well, Dudley, this fork is not to eat with. It is made to lift hay with," he said.

"Ok," Dudley said.

"Now, one of you is going to be hooked up to this rope right here. The fork will drop from that pulley up there and go down to the hay wagon. I will close it around the hay with these levers you see here on the fork. Then you will pull forward on the rope and lift the hay up into the barn. I will trip the fork and it will drop the hay into the barn. Do you boys think that we can handle that?" Farmer Dan asked.

"Oh yeah," Dudley said.

"Sure," Simon Slick said.

"So. Who goes first?" Farmer Dan asked.

"I will," Dudley said.

"Ok, here we go!" Farmer Dan said.

Paul tied the rope to a single-tree and hooked the pulling chains on each side of Dudley's hips and fastened them to the single-tree.

Dudley waited until he heard Farmer Dan say, "go!" and Paul led him forward, pulling the fork full of hay up into the barn.

Farmer Dan dropped the hay.

They did this until the wagon was empty.

They returned to the field to get another load of hay.

In a few days all the hay was safe in the barn. Then they rested until there was more work.

One morning when they all went to eat, Farmer Dan was at the barn.

"Hello there!" Farmer Dan said.

"Good morning!" Dudley and Simon Slick said at the same time.

"I was out, walking in the field yesterday afternoon. The vegetables are ready to be gathered. I know that this is short notice. Would you all like to work today?" Farmer Dan asked.

"Yes!" they all said at the same time.

"Ok. Meet me here after breakfast," Farmer Dan said.

The animals hurried and ate and got a drink of water. They went to the barn and waited for Farmer Dan.

There were vegetables all over the fields.

Daisy, Dudley, and Simon Slick hauled cucumbers to the house. Potatoes were dug and put in the cellar. Tomatoes, corn, squash, and beans by the bushels were hauled up to the house. Pumpkins were hauled and put in the smoke house. Peppers and eggplant were taken to the house.

"Come up here and bring all your friends by the fence," Mary told Dudley one afternoon. "I have some treats for you," she added.

"Watermelon?" Dudley asked.

"No, not yet. They will be ready soon. There are still a lot of vegetables in the fields, with all the late crops that are to come in yet," Mary said.

"There is still a lot of work to do yet," Dudley said.

Dudley gathered everyone up including Beth, Cotton, and Little Joe. They all marched up the hill.

The animals had cucumber peelings and pieces, strawberries, and apple and peach scraps. The animals liked that!

"We are having a ball eating all this stuff and the Harvest Ball isn't even here yet!" Dudley said.

One day Dudley said, "We need something to do to pass the time when we are not working."

"Let's take a walk to the back field and see what is going on back there," Daisy said.

"Alright," Dudley said.

Daisy, Dudley, Simon Slick, Beth, Cotton, and Little Joe all went to the back field.

Beautiful clover was growing everywhere. Daisy, Dudley, Simon Slick, and Beth began to eat.

"Yum! This is good!" Beth said.

Little Joe and Cotton were running and playing, so no one noticed where they went until Little Joe came running and yelling, "Something is wrong with Cotton!" Little Joe said.

"Where? Where?" Beth asked and ran after Little Joe.

Everyone else ran along behind them.

Cotton was lying under the apple tree heaving for breath. Beth pushed him up but he fell back down.

Dudley ran over and sat down near Cotton and said, "Do that again."

Beth pushed Cotton up and Dudley wrapped his front feet around Cotton and pressed on his stomach. An apple popped out of Cotton's mouth. Cotton took several long breaths.

Beth looked at Dudley. "You saved my baby! Thank you, Dudley!" she said.

Everyone watched as Beth licked and rubbed Cotton.

"My throat hurts," Cotton said.

"Well, let's get you back to the barn," Beth said.

They all went back to the barn, except for Dudley. He went up by the fence at Farmer Joe's house.

Farmer Joe saw him and came outside.

Dudley told him what had happened to Cotton. "I was so scared, Farmer Joe! I don't know how I knew what to do!" Dudley said.

"Dudley, what you did was called performing the "Heimlich Maneuver". Air comes from Cotton's stomach and pushes the apple out of his throat. People do that, too," Farmer Joe said.

"Will Cotton be alright now?" Dudley asked.

"Oh, yes. His throat may be sore for a while, but he should be just fine," Farmer Joe said.

"Alright, I will tell Beth," Dudley said.

"Dudley, you and all your friends need to be ready. Tomorrow is when the guests are arriving for the Harvest Ball," Farmer Joe said.

"Ok, Farmer Joe!" Dudley said.

Dudley ran down the hill to tell the others about the Harvest Ball and to tell Beth about Cotton.

"Get ready for the harvest Ball!" Dudley said.

"Is it time already?" Daisy asked.

"Everyone arrives tomorrow," Dudley said.

Everyone began to yell, "Yay! Yay!

"Oh, Beth, Farmer Joe said that Cotton may have a sore throat, but don't worry, he will be fine," Dudley said.

They all took a bath in the big lake and lay down under the stars.

"I am not going to like it when winter comes and there is nothing to do," Simon Slick said.

"I won't either," Dudley said.

None of them slept much that night.

They were all sleeping soundly the next morning when Dudley awoke.

He jumped to his feet and yelled, "It's time for the Harvest Ball!"

Dudley's Grand Harvest Ball

Beth heard Dudley yell all the way to the barn.

"It's time for the Harvest Ball!" Dudley yelled.

All the animals rushed to eat and gathered by the fence beside Farmer Joe's house.

Mary had a beautiful, long table sitting in the yard. The cloth was red and white with gold leaves on it.

Before long they heard the hooves of horses coming. "Clippity-clop, clippity-clop."

"Here they come!" Dudley said.

Three covered wagons turned and came up Farmer Joe's drive. When they got closer Dudley asked, "What does it say on that wagon?"

"The Tennessee Hillbilly," Daisy said.

"Wow!" Dudley said.

People began to climb out of the wagons everywhere, girls and boys, men and women.

Farmer Dan took their wagons and horses and mules and put them in the field.

Then came three more wagons. The writing on the first wagon said, "The Georgia Trader."

People jumped out everywhere and began to hug and kiss and some shook hands with others.

Farmer Dan took their wagons and horses and mules and one little jenny and put them in the field.

They all watched as "The Kentucky Wanderer came up the drive.

"Is this everyone, Farmer Joe?" Dudley asked.

"No. We have two more groups of guests, then everyone will be here," Farmer Joe said.

Dudley saw three more wagons coming up the drive. The writing on the first wagon said, "The Arkansas Traveler", Dudley read aloud.

Then one large, lonely wagon came up the drive. Everyone stopped and looked on as it came to a halt. Dudley knew this was someone very important by the way everyone stood so still and watched. He saw a chair on wheels lifted down from the wagon. He looked at the man who sat in it. "Farmer Malachi?" Dudley asked.

Farmer Malachi heard him and looked up. He rolled down to the fence. Everyone was silent.

"You have to be Dudley!" Farmer Malachi said.

"Yes," Dudley said.

"I have heard a lot about you. Thank you, Dudley, Farmer Malachi said.

Farmer Malachi and Dudley both cleared their throat at the same time.

"I am proud to have asked for this Harvest Ball," Dudley said.

"I am proud of you, Dudley," Farmer Malachi said.

Everyone was silent for a long moment.

Then Farmer Joe said, "What time is it, Dudley?"

"It's time for the grandest ball of all! The Grand Harvest Ball!" Dudley was so excited that he didn't even sound like himself!

"Yea! Yea! Yea!" everyone cheered.

Farmer Malachi was rolled to the head of the table.

Everyone knew each other and they were all talking and laughing.

Mary Brown and several of the women were carrying food and placing it on the long table.

Farmer Dan asked Dudley to show all the animals to the big lake for a drink of water. Dudley took the lead and they all followed him to the big lake.

Simon Slick had his eyes on the little jenny that had come to the Harvest Ball with The Georgia Trader.

"Boy, I feel young again," Simon Slick said.

"And I see why you feel young again, Simon Slick! You'd better behave yourself!" Dudley said.

"Oh, I will," Simon Slick said.

Dudley went back up to the fence with Daisy.

A big, tall man came over to the fence. "Hey, Dudley, Daisy. I am the Arkansas Traveler. I have heard a lot about the two of you," he said.

"Good to meet you," Dudley and Daisy said at the same time.

"I will be assigning dance partners for the square dance and I will lead the song for the dance," The Arkansas Traveler said.

"I don't know how to square dance," Dudley said.

"Aw, it's easy. I will tell you what to do in the song to the dance," The Arkansas Traveler said.

"You talk like Farmer Joe. You don't talk different at all," Daisy said.

"You mean like a hillbilly?" The Arkansas Traveler said.

They all had a good laugh.

"Let me tell you about myself. When I was young, I heard about the state of Arkansas. When I grew up, I began to travel there. I was born here in Tennessee. But I loved Arkansas so much that I went there and decided to stay," The Arkansas Traveler said.

"Oh. I see. I could never leave Farmer Joe's farm," Daisy said.

"Me neither," Dudley said.

"Well, that settles things. I was going to make an offer to Farmer Joe for the two of you, but if you are happy here, that's good enough for me," The Arkansas Traveler said.

"Gather around everyone! It is time to eat!" Farmer Joe announced.

Everyone gathered around the table.

"Farmer Malachi looked at Dudley and said, "I hear that you say Grace over the food, so go ahead, Dudley."

Dudley paused for a long moment and looked around at everyone. Then he bowed his head and said, "God, we thank you for the food and all of our friends that are here today. And, may we have the best Harvest Ball of all," Dudley said.

When Dudley looked up he saw tears in Farmer Malachi's eyes.

"Thank you, Dudley. You're the most wonderful mule that I have ever met! But, I will call you, Dudley," Farmer Malachi said. Farmer Malachi flashed Dudley a big smile.

At that moment Dudley knew that Farmer Joe had told Farmer Malachi everything about him, and he was proud. He stood up straight and held his head high.

"Thank you, Farmer Malachi for all that you've done for Farmer Joe. I am sure that I wouldn't be on this farm today if not for you," Dudley said.

Dudley was crying. He didn't care. They were tears of joy. He reached over and kissed Daisy because she was crying too.

A truck backed up to the gate and Farmer Dan got out. "Dudley, gather everyone up for me," Farmer Dan said.

Farmer Dan and some of the other men began to throw watermelons over the fence.

Dudley, Daisy, Simon Slick, and his jenny friend, and all the other animals ate until they were full.

All the people ate until they were full.

Farmer Joe announced that everyone should rest until the fun all began at supper time.

Everyone rested for a while.

Farmer Dan had built shower stalls for the men to take their showers.

The ladies and children took turns bathing.

Everyone put on their best dance clothes.

When supper time came and everyone gathered around the table, Dudley and Daisy were the first ones to the fence.

"Wow!" Dudley said. "Look at those ladies' hair!"

"That lady over there had better watch out if a bee comes along! It might think that her hair is a nest," Daisy said. "Look at that dress she has on. If I were a person, I would love to wear that. It is beautiful!"

The lady turned and looked at Dudley and Daisy and came walking over to the fence. "Daisy, Dudley, my name is Allie. I am very proud to meet you," she said. "My hairdo is called a Bee-hive." She laughed and reached out and scratched Daisy on the nose. "You would be beautiful in my dress, even as a mule!" Allie said.

"Thank you," Daisy said.

"Who did you come to the ball with?" Dudley asked.

"I am Farmer Malachi's nurse at the rest home. Farmer Joe hired me to come and take care of him," Allie said.

"If I were a person, I would want you for my nurse, too," Dudley said.

"Thank you, Dudley. Now, I had better go and check on Farmer Malachi," Allie said.

About that time Farmer Joe said, "gather 'round everyone! Let's eat! Then the games and dances will begin!"

All the people ate and enjoyed the food from the big table.

The animals had corn pudding.

"Boy! That is good!" Dudley said.

"Oh yes!" Daisy said as she licked her mouth.

The Arkansas Traveler paired everyone up in couples including the animals. Then he asked for four couples to demonstrate the dance routine to the ones who didn't know it. Four couples came forward. "Let the music begin," he said.

"Hold hands with your partner now, promenade, around the ring we go! Turn back now, promenade her back again! Swing your partner, then do-se-do! Then promenade around the ring again! Swing your partner to the right! Swing your partner to the left! Then promenade and back again! Change partners to the right and stop!

"Wow! Can we do that, Daisy?" Dudley said.

"I don't know but I am going to try," Daisy said.

"Ok! Everyone get with your partner and get ready," The Arkansas Traveler said.

The music began and Dudley and Daisy put their heads together and promenaded around the ring.

All the other animals did the same.

The Arkansas Traveler said, "Swing your partner to the right!"

Dudley and Daisy hooked their necks to the right and swung around in a circle.

"Swing your partner to the left!" the Arkansas Traveler said.

Dudley and Daisy hooked their necks and around in a circle they went.

"This is fun!" Daisy said.

"Yeah!" Dudley said.

They do-se-doed and promenaded. In a circle they all went.

"And change partners!" The Arkansas Traveler said.

Everyone changed partners.

They danced until Daisy and Dudley were partners again. The Arkansas Traveler stopped everyone and said, "Now everyone have some drinks and snacks over at the table and rest."

"Boy! I like this!" Dudley said.

"I do too!" Daisy said.

Dudley and Daisy went and joined an apple bobbing contest. The animals got to eat the apples when the contest was done.

It was getting late and some of them were going to bed.

Farmer Joe, Farmer Dan, Farmer Malachi, and The Georgia Trader were sitting on the patio talking.

"Dudley, I want to sleep here next to the fence. I don't want to miss anything!" Daisy said.

"Ok, Daisy. I don't want to miss anything either." Dudley said.

Dudley wasn't tired enough to sleep. He was still excited about finding out what they would do tomorrow. He lay by the fence listening to the men talking.

"Dudley and Daisy were the best square dancers in the field tonight," Farmer Joe said.

"Yes, they were! Simon Slick was trying too hard! He was busy trying to impress that little jenny," Farmer Dan said.

"Yes he was," Farmer Joe said.

"Did you see Simon Slick sling that little mule so hard by the neck that she fell?" The Georgia Trader said.

"I sure did! I am going to have a talk with him tomorrow," Farmer Joe said.

"What will they do tomorrow when they have to do the slow dancing?" Farmer Dan asked.

"Oh, that's just going to be what Simon Slick ordered, when he finds out!" Farmer Joe said.

"What is slow dancing?" Daisy asked.

"I don't know, but it sounds nice," Dudley said.

"I can't wait to find out!" Daisy said.

Daisy fell asleep.

Dudley looked at Daisy and said, "talk about falling asleep talking! She just did!"

Dudley thought about the slow dancing. He imagined everyone square dancing in slow motion. It was a pitiful sight! "It can't be," Dudley said to himself. "I will just have to wait and see, he said.

Dudley thought about the cold winter ahead. Suddenly he saw he and Daisy, Beth, and Simon Slick, Cotton, and Little Joe down in the barnyard, square dancing. Dudley said out loud, "Maybe it won't be such a long winter after all. We can practice for next year," he said. He heard Farmer Joe talking.

"My animals are the best. I can just tell them not to do something and they listen to me," Farmer Joe said.

"I wish I was young again and could live here and see all this," Farmer Malachi said.

"So do I," Farmer Dan said.

"It is something to see!" Farmer Joe said.

Mary came out and asked if she could get them anything before she went to bed.

They all asked for iced tea.

Mary brought each of them a nice, tall glass of tea with a lemon wedge on the side of the glass.

Dudley fell asleep listening to them talk about animal trading.

They all went to bed soon after Dudley fell asleep.

The next morning Dudley awoke to a sound that he hadn't heard in a long time.

A rooster was sitting on a post near Dudley's head. "Cock-a-doodle-do!" He said.

"Who are you?" Dudley asked.

"My name is Domino," he said.

"Where did you come from?" Dudley asked.

"From Kentucky! I am a present to Farmer Joe from the Kentucky Wanderer. I grew up on his farm," Domino said.

"Welcome home!" Dudley said.

"Domino began to cry. "I just hope that Farmer Joe is as good to me as The Kentucky Wanderer has been!" Domino cried.

"Oh, don't worry! He will be!" Dudley said.

"Ok. Gotta go!' Domino said.

Domino took off and ran to the gate and began to eat seeds from the watermelons that were eaten the night before.

Everyone began to get out of bed.

Breakfast was served on the long table.

Apples were thrown across the gate for all the animals to have a special treat.

The games all started after breakfast.

They played horse shoes and Pin the Tail on the Donkey. They had a watermelon throwing contest that Simon Slick won. Then they bobbed for apples until they were all tired.

They rested for a while.

Before they knew it, day turned into evening. It was time for supper.

Potato salad and creamed corn was on the long table. Dudley watched the ladies carry dish after dish out and place them on the long table. All the time he kept looking at the corn and potato salad.

The Kentucky Wanderer saw what he was looking at and brought he and Daisy a plate full of it.

"Yum, yum! This is good!" Dudley said.

"It sure is!" Daisy said.

"Thank you!" they both said at the same time.

"We have to keep our best couple dancing, don't we?" the Kentucky Wanderer said.

"We sure do!" Dudley said.

He patted both of them on the head and went to ask for a couple to demonstrate the slow dancing. The couple slow danced and then demonstrated The Fox Trot. Everyone joined in and began to dance.

A stallion that came with The Arkansas Traveler kept asking Daisy to dance. Daisy didn't want to be rude so she kept dancing with him.

Dudley was worried about Daisy so he cut in several times.

The stallion just kept coming back. Finally the stallion told Dudley, "leave her alone. She's with me. I'm dancing with her tonight."

"No she is not yours! She is mine! And you had better leave her alone!" Dudley said.

Dudley turned around and it appeared that he was walking away.

The stallion told Daisy, "look at that! He's just a big ole chicken!"

About that time Dudley kicked up his heels and kicked the stallion right in the teeth.

The stallion ran off.

Farmer Joe came over to the fence. "What did you do that for, Dudley," he asked.

"Because he was being rude to Daisy!" Dudley said.

"Well, Dudley, we don't use violence on this farm," Farmer Joe said.

The music had stopped and everyone was looking at Dudley and Farmer Joe.

"I am sorry, Farmer Joe. I am sorry everyone," Dudley said.

The Arkansas Traveler came walking over.

"It's ok, Dudley. Sometimes Pride gets out of line. He will behave himself now," The Arkansas Traveler said.

"Ok! Let's dance!" Farmer Joe said.

Farmer Joe patted Dudley on the nose. When Dudley looked at Farmer Joe, he knew that everything was fine again.

They danced until way into the night before some of them began to go to bed.

When they were dancing the last dance for the night Daisy and Dudley had their heads together. They were twirling around like a slow dream. Dudley said, "I love you, Daisy!"

They were quiet for a moment.

"Tomorrow is the last day and everyone goes home," Dudley said.

"I know. It seems so sad," Daisy said.

"It is sad. We are going to miss all this when it is gone," Dudley said.

Dudley and Daisy were up by the fence first thing the next morning. Everyone got up early that morning.

Food was carried out and placed on the long table. The Kentucky Wanderer was making flap-jacks on a large grill.

Dudley asked Mary about a dish that she had placed on the table.

"Oh, that is my special spinach and mushroom omelet," Mary said.

Mary gave Dudley a taste.

"Yum! That is good!" Dudley said.

"We are going to miss you, Mary," Daisy said.

Everyone ate until they were full.

The animals had corn pudding and apples.

"May I have you attention please," Farmer Joe said. "For those of you who do not know this, The Georgia Trader is going to perform a wedding ceremony," Farmer Joe announced.

Farmer Joe turned around and knelt down in front of Mary. "Mary, will you marry me?" he asked.

Mary was crying until she could not speak.

Everyone held their breath.

Finally she spoke. "Yes! I have waited over half my life for this moment!" Mary said.

The air erupted out of everyone's lungs and ended up as a great big cheer.

Farmer Joe started to get off his knees but couldn't get up. "I look like getting married!" he said.

" I can't even get up!"

Everyone began to laugh. The laughter got harder and faster until Farmer Joe began to laugh at himself.

The Georgia Trader and The Arkansas Traveler lifted Farmer Joe to his feet.

Everyone began to laugh again and clap their hands.

The animals cheered loudly.

"Oh. Where did we get to?" Farmer Joe said.

"Simon Slick has asked to marry his new love, Cindy, and she will be living here on the farm with us," Farmer Joe said.

A cheer went up for Simon Slick and Cindy.

"Beth has fallen in love with a longhorn bull from Texas that The Arkansas Traveler brought me as a gift," Farmer Joe said.

Another cheer went up for them.

"One last thing, Farmer Malachi has decided to live here on the farm for the remainder of his life," Farmer Joe said.

Another cheer went up for Farmer Malachi.

"I have hired a nurse to take care of Farmer Malachi," Farmer Joe said.

Dudley looked over at Farmer Malachi. He was looking back at Dudley. They made eye contact, and at that moment Dudley knew that he had given Farmer Malachi a whole new reason to live.

Dudley nodded a "welcome home" to Farmer Malachi.

Farmer Malachi nodded a "thank you" to Dudley.

"Are there any more announcements?" Farmer Joe asked.

"Yes," Farmer Dan said. Farmer Dan turned to Farmer Malachi's nurse and got down on his knees. "Allie, will you marry me?" he asked.

Allie put her arms around his neck and said, "I sure will!"

"Alright!" Farmer Dan said.

Everyone clapped and cheered. Dudley and Daisy were jumping up and down with happiness.

Farmer Joe paused a moment to see if there was anything else to be said. Just when he started to speak, Daisy spoke.

"Farmer Joe, I have an announcement to make," Daisy said.

Daisy looked at Dudley. "Dudley and I are going to be parents next March!" she said.

"We are? We are!" Dudley said.

"Yes, we are!" Daisy said.

Dudley jumped up and down. "We are!" he said. He jumped along the fence and back. "We are!" he said. Dudley began to try to hold down his excitement.

Farmer Joe stood there. His mouth fell open. People began to cheer until they saw his reaction and they stopped.

Farmer Joe said, "Wow! Two mules!"

When everyone understood what was going on, they began to cheer loudly.

Dudley kissed Daisy and said, "I can't wait to see my son!"

"Congratulations to the both of you!" Farmer Joe said.

But, they didn't hear him.

Farmer Joe said, "Ok! Arkansas Traveler, you lead the games and the dance today."

So, The Arkansas Traveler lined everyone up to start the watermelon throwing contest. They threw watermelons, and bobbed apples, and pinned the tail on the donkey, threw horse shoes and even played "Red Rover". The Arkansas Traveler called for a break right before supper.

"This day sure did pass fast and I hoped that it would never end," Dudley said.

"Well, Dudley, we already know that The Harvest Ball is a time for hopes and dreams to come true," Farmer Joe said.

"You never know what might happen," Daisy said.

"That is true. We will see what happens," Dudley said.

The ladies were carrying large containers of food out to the long table.

"That looks good," Dudley said. What is that, Farmer Joe?"

Farmer Joe was taking a large bowl from Mary. "This is coleslaw," Farmer Joe said.

"What is that over there, Farmer Joe?" Daisy asked.

"That is banana pudding and this one here beside it is strawberry pudding," Farmer Joe said.

"Yum!" Dudley said.

"That all sounds good and looks good!" Daisy said.

"Mary gave me a banana once," Dudley said.

"She did?" Farmer Joe asked.

"Yes, and it was good!" Dudley said.

"Well, I'd better go and help with the food," Farmer Joe said.

Dudley and Daisy got so hungry looking at and smelling all the food that their bellies began to growl.

Mary announced that if there was anything left that the animals could have it.

"That's one dream come true!" Dudley said.

When the food was placed in a large bin Dudley and Daisy were the first ones there to eat.

All the other animals complained that they didn't want human food. They wanted corn and fresh hay.

Farmer Dan and some of the men went down to the barn and put out corn and fresh hay for them.

The big stallion stayed at the other end of the bin eating.

A little boy who came with the Kentucky Wanderer got something out of a bowl that was left on the table and came over to the gate.

The stallion looked up.

The little boy said, "You're a mighty, big stallion! What is your name?"

"Pride," the stallion answered. "What is yours?"

"Arthur," the little boy said. "I'd say you are so strong that you could do anything!"

"Hum. Is that a fact?" Pride said.

"I brought you something," Arthur said.

He held out his hand.

"Me? You brought that to me?" Pride asked.

Pride reached over and grabbed the object and began to chew. He let out a yell. "Yeow!" Pride yelled. He spit and yelled "yeow!" again and took off for the big lake, jumping like a rabbit.

Pride was still yelling "yeow, yeow!" he said.

Everyone was looking around and trying to figure out what was going on.

The Kentucky Wanderer came running over.

"Arthur, what did you do?" The Kentucky Wanderer asked.

Arthur didn't answer.

"When you are around, trouble always seems to follow you," The Kentucky Wanderer said.

Arthur looked down at his feet.

"I gave Pride a hot pepper," Arthur said.

"Why did you do that?" the Kentucky Wanderer asked.

"Because, Farmer Joe told me to be careful. He said that they were one thousand times hotter than anything I had ever tasted. I just wanted to see how hot they were," Arthur answered.

"Ok. You go to bed now. Then tomorrow morning you tell me if you learned anything else!" The Kentucky Wanderer said.

Simon Slick came walking up and said, "excuse me. Pride is down by the creek mumbling something. And the big lake is full of soap. And he wants The Arkansas Traveler to take him away. He says that he doesn't want to see this place again. He is crying his eyes out!"

Everyone was quiet for a moment.

"Pride will be ok. He just had his pride damaged a little bit," The Arkansas Traveler said.

Everyone began to laugh. The laughter was heard at the next farm down the road.

"For a man in Farmer Joe's condition, he sure is having a big shindig over there," the neighbor farmer said.

Farmer Joe announced that it was time to perform the weddings among the animals. "It is time for Beth and Rob Bert to become a family!" he said.

"What kind of name is that, Farmer Joe?" Dudley asked.

"Well, the story is that he started out as Rob. One day at a rodeo he saw a man with a billfold on a chain in his pocket. He hung the chain on his horn and robbed the man as a joke. But the joke turned on him. The man's name was Bert. So everyone started teasing him and calling him Rob Bert," Farmer Joe explained.

"That is funny!" Daisy said, laughing.

Everyone began to laugh.

Beth spoke up. "Alright! Let's everyone be respectful here! We have decided to call him Robert. Isn't that a pretty name?" Beth asked.

"Yes, Beth, it is. Robert it will be," Farmer Joe said.

"Simon Slick, you and Cindy get ready to get married. Are there any more animals that wish to be married?" Farmer Joe asked.

No other animals spoke up.

Farmer Joe said, "I give you, The Georgia Trader!"

"Good evening everyone. We are gathered here to wed our friends Beth and Robert and Simon Slick and Cindy. Is there anyone here who can show just cause as to why either of these two couples should not wed? Speak now or forever hold your peace!" The Georgia Trader said.

Everyone was quiet for a moment.

Daisy started crying. She got louder and louder.

"What's wrong, Daisy?" Farmer Joe asked.

"Simon Slick and Beth won't be spending time with us anymore!" Daisy answered.

"Yes they will. They are going to be just like you and Dudley," Farmer Joe said.

"In that case, I am happy for them! I am sorry," Daisy said.

"Oh. I assume everything is ok," The Georgia trader said.

He paused for a moment.

"Simon Slick, and Robert, do you take these two beautiful animals for your wives?" The Georgia Trader asked.

Simon Slick said, "I do."

Robert said, "I do."

"And do you, Cindy, and Beth, take these two beautiful animals for your husbands?"

"I do," Cindy said.

"I do," Beth said.

"Simon Slick and Cindy, I now pronounce you husband and wife!"

Simon Slick and Cindy kissed.

Simon Slick was so excited that after he kissed Cindy, that he kissed Beth.

"Simon Slick, we didn't get married!" Beth said.

"Oh, that's right!" Simon Slick said.

Everyone laughed and cheered for the two couples.

Farmer Joe and Mary and Farmer Dan and Allie all stood together on the lawn.

"Look at Farmer Joe and Farmer Dan. They look good in those fancy new suits they have on," Dudley said.

"Look at Mary. She is beautiful!" Daisy said.

"Allie doesn't look bad either," Dudley said.

"We are gathered here today in the sight of God, and these witnesses to join these couples in matrimony," The Georgia Trader said.

"Did he say macaroni? But we ate that!" Dudley said.

Everyone laughed loudly.

Farmer Joe and Mary danced out into the yard, with Farmer Dan and Allie right behind them.

After the dance was over, a big cake was brought out and cut. Everyone got a piece, including the animals.

After everyone was in bed Dudley and Daisy lay by the fence.

"The Harvest Ball is over," Dudley said with a long face.

"I know. It is a whole year until the next one," Daisy said.

"Yes, and everyone is leaving tomorrow," Dudley said.

Daisy went to sleep.

Dudley dozed off when it was nearly morning.

Dudley woke to the sound of people talking. He sprang to his feet.

"Daisy, Daisy! Wake up! Everyone is gathered for breakfast and they will be leaving soon!" Dudley said.

Farmer Malachi bowed his head. "God, we thank you for a wonderful harvest ball. Keep our friends safe as they begin their journeys home," Farmer Malachi prayed.

Everyone ate in silence.

Everyone said their goodbyes after breakfast. There were hugs and kisses and tears shed then everyone loaded into the wagons.

Mary gave each wagon a basket of fried chicken, potatoes and biscuits to eat on their trip home.

The wagons headed down the drive, the Georgia Trader, then The Kentucky Wanderer, and the Tennessee Hillbilly in the back of the line.

All the animals ran along the fence saying, "bye! See you next year!" until they were gone.

All the animals sat by the fence for a long while after they were gone.

Then Dudley led them to the barn to assign stables for the winter.

Long into the winter, Farmer Malachi heard a noise. He looked out the sliding glass door toward the barn.

"Well, I'll be! Look at this, Farmer Joe!" Farmer Malachi said.

Farmer Joe came over and looked out the door.

The animals were square- dancing in the barn yard!

"Practicing for next year!" Farmer Joe said.

They both watched in silence for a few moments.

"I would say that you are happy to see that," Farmer Joe said.

"I wouldn't change a thing! I have a feeling that this winter is not going to be as long and cold after all! Things like this sure does warm this old cold heart of mine!" Farmer Malachi said.

Dear Reader,

I hope that you enjoy reading this book as much as I have enjoyed creating it.

More to come with these characters.

About the Author:

Ellen Sherwood lives with her husband in a small town in East Tennessee. She is very busy with her writing. This is her second book.

She enjoys cooking and sewing and gardening. Sometimes she enjoys curling up on the couch with a good novel by John Grisham, her favorite author.